POSSESSING JOY

A Secret to Strength & Longevity

By Steve Backlund

This book is dedicated to:
Caden, my grandson - for thinking I am funny
Jerry Frost - for mentoring me to a higher place
Richard & Jeanie Waters - for making Christianity real
Joy Hale - for serving and supporting me faithfully

Acknowledgements
Joy "Consultants" for This Book: Paul Barela, Loyd Golleher, Dan Hale, Dale Kaz, Gerard Kaz, Tom Osterday, Jill Perry, Sue Scott, Suki Smith, Ted Smith, Emil Swift and Lorraine West. Special thanks to Lorraine West for her detailed assistance in this book's contents. In addition to these, Wendy Backlund has been my chief advisor for Possessing Joy.

Front and Back Cover Design: Linda Lee

ISBN 978-0-9854773-2-5

Forward
by
Georgian Banov

*C*oping with the complexities of a stressed-out world all around us can be overwhelming at times. As chronic "looks of anxiety" threaten to dominate our facial landscape, Steve Backlund's book, Possessing Joy is an effective dose of anti-depression medication delivering a potent message on the sheer simplicity of joy. Just like those strategic Gatorade stations along the path of a grueling triathlon offer much needed liquid replenishments, this "little paper cup" of a book pours out a desperately needed drink – a divine endurance formula which will arrest the joy-depleting fatigue that is plaguing so many of the long distance-runners in the Body of Christ today.

But before anybody quickly dismisses it as just another book on the "principle" of joy, these pages should be thoroughly read and given a chance to sink in. It is about an actual substance. It is a drink and it is an anointing. The joy of the LORD, which when taken in, is the very core strength that sustains and enables us to supernaturally endure the hardships of an otherwise unendurable race. Unless our spiritual mentors have properly raised us to drink from the same "Rock that followed them, and that Rock was Christ," we will find ourselves spiritually dehydrated and exhausted well before the finish line.

Moving past the notion that joy is just a code or idyllic rule to live by, the saints are beginning to rediscover that, after all, in His presence there is fullness of joy. It is based upon a deep and intimate, all-sustaining love relationship with Jesus who was "anointed with the oil of gladness"; and, which in turn, makes our hearts very glad.

And so, it is really about love. It is about being constrained, ruled, overmastered and so possessed by the love of Christ that, regardless of the circumstances, joy always spills over.

Abandoned lovers are consumed by an unyielding passionate pursuit of the object of their love. God Himself is the epitome of perfect and holy lover. He reveals His pursuit of fallen humankind in an open display: the fury of a Father who abandoned His own Son to the cruelest and most undeserved punishment, a shameful death on a cross. In fact, it pleased Him to bruise Him. God, who in order to reveal His hiddenness to a humanity blinded by sin, had to expose the nakedness of His Son's crucified body, paying the fathomless price of our redemption, thorough and complete. This is the fundamental belief supporting the message of this book, enabling us to draw with joy from the deep well of our salvation.

Like Father, like son and daughter; powerful duo Steve and Wendy Backlund are relentless in their delivery. They open up for us in full view the contagious joy of our Heavenly Father who has defeated His enemy on the battleground of Calvary and who is now populating the earth with His ever-growing family.

Possessing Joy is a powerful eight-week study on the topic of joy. Steve, as a former athletic coach, provides the essential ingredients for a life-long, joy-filled journey for every believer. He also cleverly reminds all of us to avoid the trap of joylessness in our spiritual warfare, lest we start to take on the character of the very enemy we are trying to wrestle.

As forty day fasts are gaining popularity and have become frequent events among charismatics and evangelicals alike, this devotional study by Steve Backlund would be the best 40 day "frown-fast" manual around.

Thank you Steve for keeping us on track. Well done! One small request though for next time, could you expand your terrific manual of joy devotionals into 365 joy devotionals, and translate them into every major world language, as Christian mentors throughout the nations desperately need it?

Georgian A. Banov
Founder of Global Celebration

Table of Contents

Eight Weeks (56 Days) to Possess Joy

Table of Contents Continued
Eight Weeks (56 Days) to Possess Joy

About The Author

Steve Backlund is known for his wisdom and practical insights on "how to do life." The students in our ministry school - - Bethel School of Supernatural Ministry - love him because he always leaves them encouraged and refreshed in their vision. He has an unusual gift to take the mundane and make it exciting, and to take the familiar and make it new. **Bill Johnson; Bethel Church; Redding, CA - Author of *When Heaven Invades Earth***

Steve Backlund is a credible source for the transforming power of the joy of the Holy Spirit. I've personally witnessed this metamorphosis take place in Steve's life over the past six years, and I can attest to the exponential increase of his genuine love for Jesus and breakthrough anointing for the people he pastors throughout the Northwest. If you are tired of the stifling confines of the cocoon of mediocre Christianity, join Steve in this eight-week joy devotional and watch your own life take wings on the wind of the Father's delight. **Dan McCollam, Director of the International Worship Arts Recording Schools**

****

If you enjoy this book
go to ignitedhope.com:

- For CD teachings that will inspire faith and hope
- For sermon downloads of recent messages by Steve or Wendy
- For information on the Backlund's upcoming speaking itinerary
- To contact Steve or Wendy about speaking to your group
- For many free helps to inspire your life

Read Steve and Wendy Backlund's first book, *Igniting Faith in 40 Days*, a devotional ideal for a 40 Day Negativity Fast. It will ignite your hope which, in turn, will cause your faith to go to the next level. Also, Steve has authored <u>Cracks in the Foundation</u> (see back of this book for more information about <u>Cracks in the Foundation</u>.

How to Use This Book

There are three main ways to read *Possessing Joy*:

- ❖ An eight-week personal or family devotional

- ❖ An eight-week group study

- ❖ A "quick read" that you read over and over to get its truths deep into your life

Special Features of *Possessing Joy*:

- ❖ A Daily Devotional that shares the biblical priority of joy

- ❖ A Declaration to speak at the end of each devotional that will help create a positive "joy stronghold" *

- ❖ Information on the Health Benefits of Laughter (Day 6 of each week)

- ❖ Review Assignments and Questions (Day 7 of each week)

Final Suggestions in Reading *Possessing Joy*:

- ❖ Know that God never commands us to do something we cannot do. We can be joyful. God will do it in us.

- ❖ Don't be critical of those who do not seem joyful. It won't help the joy process.

- ❖ Rejoice with those who are more joyful than you. Laugh with those who laugh. It will stir joy in you.

- ❖ Know that deep joy results from a revelation of God's goodness, love and promises.

* See appendix for teaching on the power of declaring truth.

Possessing Joy

Week One

DAY #1 *A Merry Heart is Good Like a Medicine*

Imagine being prescribed medication and the pharmacist tells you, "Take this three times a day for ten days and you will get better." Most of us would start taking the medication because we would believe it would work. This faith, mixed with the medication, has helped many to get well.

"Dr. God" has given us a prescription that has tremendous potential for our strength, health, energy level, longevity, and mental clarity; it's called "a merry heart." Those who heed the "Great Physician" and mix their faith with the joy of the Lord will start on a wonderful journey toward vitality in life.

This book is designed to ignite your joy. Some would object and say, "That's fine for you, but I am not a joyful person." In response to this, please consider two things.

First, can you imagine someone saying, "I can't be loving because I am not a loving person." We would say, "That's ridiculous. We are commanded to love. God would never tell us to do something we could not do" (I John 4:7-11). The same principle holds true for joy. Each of us has the power and ability to become abundantly joyful. It is a "muscle" that can be developed in our lives.

Secondly, this writer was entrenched in a joyless state that resulted from an "it's not my personality" belief. Instead of using God's word to create my identity, I was using my past and my experience to tell me who I was. As I will share later in this book, I was delivered from this bondage and my joy was increased dramatically. It can happen to you, too.

Dr. God is telling us to take our "good medicine." He is urging us to make joy and laughter a big part of our overall plan for good health for our lives. This spiritual truth is supported by science and recent medical research. So, let's take our medicine. We won't be sorry we did.

Declaration: A merry heart is good medicine. I "take" this prescription of joy and laughter daily. As I do, my health and vitality are strengthened.

Feeling Guilty About Being Joyful

There is so much pain in the world that it is easy to feel bad or uncomfortable about living joyfully. "After all," we think, "how can I be happy when so many people are struggling?" Usually this conclusion comes from our own thinking, but sometimes it can result from "guilt trips" that others seemingly put on us if we are too happy. We need to recognize though that if we continually curtail our joy and optimism, we are robbing them and ourselves of a much-needed aspect of God's nature.

Shame can also hinder us from accepting full joy for our lives because we unconsciously believe that we are still unworthy and undeserving of being happy. Like a dripping faucet in the back of our soul, we judge that we deserve to suffer and be punished. This inability to fully accept our forgiveness is a big issue with many people; it blocks blessing and hope for our lives. We need a greater revelation of the Father's love that will uproot this deception that wounds us (Luke 7:47).

People around us need us to possess joy. By doing so, we are more able to set others free (and leave an inheritance of victory). Our breaking through the lies of the enemy will allow us to impart "the garment of praise for the spirit of heaviness" (Isaiah 61:3). We will bring faith to a whole new level in the lives of those we touch.

Of course, there are times we need to be sensitive to the feelings of others and "weep with those who weep", but we cannot let guilt and shame hinder us from possessing outrageous joy for our lives. If we do, then we will be restricting our strength for our journey and our influence for Christ on others. Truly, biblical joy is a catalyst to breakthrough in the kingdom of God.

Declare: I am forgiven. God loves me. The resurrection and death of Jesus has made me worthy and deserving to be happy and blessed. I am sensitive to the needs and emotions of others around me, but I still move forward in rejoicing in the Lord. My joy increasingly breaks off spirits of discouragement and heaviness all around me.

"I will be happy when _____ happens." We can fill in the blank with whatever we think is the key for our joy to begin. For example: "I will be joyful when I move out of the house, or when I get married, or when I have children, or when I get more money, or when I get a new home, or when the kids are in school, or when the kids leave home, or when I retire, or when this circumstance changes, or . . ."

The "I will be happy when" mindset is called <u>destination disease</u>. This is a malady that plagues multitudes and is rooted in the belief that joy depends on changed circumstances. Certainly circumstances play a role in our positive emotions (we cannot deny the difficulty that life can bring at certain times), but ultimately we need to find inner victory over the giants of discontent and discouragement.

Paul said, "I have <u>learned</u> in whatever state I am, to be content: I know how to be abased, and I know how to abound . . . " (Philippians 4:10-11). He learned to be inwardly successful no matter if he was prospering or if he was in lack.

Paul apparently had a season in his life when he focused on (and was *learning about*) the development of the inner <u>soul prosperity</u> of being content (3 John 2). We too need a time like this in our lives. It will never seem convenient to do so, but it is necessary in order to develop a life of joy.

Here is a truth to ponder: if we are not joyful <u>now</u>, then we will probably not be joyful <u>then</u> (when circumstances change). The root issue is in us, not in our current situations. Let's overcome destination disease and determine today to live in a new level of rejoicing and celebration in God's promises. As we do so, we will find our joy becoming a "faith weapon" to change things like never before.

Declare: I have overcome destination disease. I am learning to be content and joyful now. I am breaking through the lie that says I can only be happy if certain things change. I rejoice now in God's goodness and in His promises. I can and will be joyful now.

Jesus - Mr. Spock With Long Hair?

Many people think that Jesus was "robotic" and unemotional. He supposedly "floated" through life with a serenity and restraint that would make Maharishi Mahesh Yogi and John Wayne envious. Some picture Him like Mr. Spock from Star Trek - completely devoid of emotions, especially laughter.

Hebrews 1:8 debunks this when it says of Jesus, " . . . Your God, has anointed You with <u>the oil of gladness</u> more than Your companions." Some would say, "Well, this is speaking of Jesus when He ascended to heaven." I don't believe so (even though a "glad Jesus" in heaven would mess up many people's theology!).

John 15:11 shows that Jesus walked in great joyfulness when on earth. He said, "These things I have spoken to you, that <u>My joy</u> may remain in you, and that <u>your joy may be full</u>" (see also John 16:24; 17:13 and I John 1:4). It was a big deal to Jesus that we walk like Him in this "full joy." (And I don't believe for a moment that this gladness was always a quiet, inner joy that looked like Mr. Spock. I believe it was at times noisy, silly, freeing and made Jesus fun to be with.)

Unlike our Savior, many Christians today are not fun to be with. Jesus was the desired guest at weddings and other events that "sinners" were attending. His joy caused Him to be attractive and have favor in relationships. He set an example for us to not only live in an uncompromising manner in the world, but to do so with joy.

There's one more thing to say about this. **It's important to realize that our mental picture concerning the personality of Jesus will dramatically affect our own personality**. Religious tradition has practically eliminated true joy from the Jesus we worship. The consequences have been unfortunate for our lives, our churches and for the kingdom. Let's seek God afresh and find the joy side of His nature that is so desperately needed today.

Declare: The Holy Spirit is making me more like Jesus every day. My emotions are getting unlocked and I am experiencing great joy. I laugh heartily every day. My joy causes many to receive hope and to come into the kingdom.

DAY #5 *He Who Sits in the Heavens Shall Laugh (Psalm 2:4)*

What is God finding so funny in heaven? "The kings of the earth set themselves, and the rulers take counsel together, against the LORD and against His Anointed, saying, 'Let us break their bonds in pieces and cast away their cords from us.' He who sits in the heavens shall laugh . . ." (Psalm 2:2-4). God is laughing at what His enemies are saying and planning.

This heavenly hilarity becomes personal for us as we pray, "Your kingdom come, your will be done, on earth as it is in heaven" (Matthew 6:10). If God is laughing at what the devil is proclaiming, then we should join our Father here on earth. (Remember, Jesus said, "I say to you, the Son can do nothing of Himself, but what He sees the Father do; for whatever He does, the Son also does in like manner" (John 5:19).

The devil is a liar and he is constantly speaking lies that are inconsistent with the promises of God (John 8:44; 2 Peter 1:4). Responding to his lies with laughter can be a powerful, liberating experience. I have led many prayer meetings where we ask, "Are you hearing any lies lately that we can laugh with you about?" One by one, people share things like: "God won't meet my needs in the future" (ha, ha); "Things are only going to get worse" (ha, ha); "No one gets healed when I pray for them" (ho, ho); "I've sinned too much to be blessed and to enjoy life" (ha, ha); "My city is hard to the gospel" (hee, hee); "God has just about had enough of me" (ha, ha); or "I'm stupid and I'm accident prone" (ha, ha). It is amazing therapy to laugh at lies. Try it.

Laughter is obviously not the only weapon that we use against the devil's deceptions and tactics, but it is what the Heavenly Father does; so let's purpose to join Him on a regular basis (and bring a little more of heaven down to earth).

Declare: I laugh uproariously when I hear a lie from the devil. God's promises are true and the devil's words are false. I am chuckling more and more as I look at Satan's lies from God's perspective.

Resolve to keep happy and your joy shall form an invincible host against difficulties. - Helen Keller

Health Benefits of Laughter

Norman Cousins is a "laughter legend" who in 1979 called attention to the medical community of the potential therapeutic effects of humor and laughter. He described his use of laughter during his treatment for ankylosing spondylitis. Because Cousins believed that negative emotions had a negative impact on health, he theorized that the opposite was also true (that positive emotions would have a positive effect on his health). He believed that laughter could open him up to feelings of joy, hope, confidence and love (and thus to healing and health.)

Cousins is probably the best known proponents of using positive emotions to improve health, but he was certainly not the first to assert this relationship. As early as the 1300s, Henri de Mondeville, a professor of surgery, wrote: "Let the surgeon take care to regulate the whole regimen of the patient's life for joy and happiness, allowing his relatives and special friends to cheer him, and by having someone tell him jokes."

The difference now is that we have scientific studies of the relationship between joy and health. Cousins himself spent the last 12 years of his life at the UCLA Medical School in the Department of Behavioral Medicine where he explored the scientific proof of his beliefs. He also established the Humor Research Task Force which coordinated and supported clinical research on humor

.

Something to laugh about (a funny pun)

A woman has twins and gives them up for adoption. One of them goes to a family in Egypt and is named "Ahmal." The other goes to a family in Spain. They name him "Juan." Years later, Juan sends a picture of himself to his birth mother. Upon receiving the picture, she tells her husband that she wishes she also had a picture of Ahmal. Her husband responds, "They're twins! If you've seen Juan, you've seen Ahmal."

THE FIVE DEVOTIONALS FROM THIS PAST WEEK
A Merry Heart is Good Like a Medicine
Feeling Guilty About Being Joyful
Destination Disease
Jesus - Mr. Spock With Long Hair?
He Who Sits in the Heavens Shall Laugh

TWO ACTIONS TO TAKE:
Read or review each of the week's five devotionals.
Read out loud each of the five declarations at the end of the devotionals.

QUESTIONS TO ASK:
Which of the five devotionals spoke to you in the greatest way? Why?
What one sentence from the five devotionals stood out to you the most? Why did this speak to you?
What two or three steps can you take this week to move forward in strengthening your life through joy?

FURTHER ACTIONS TO TAKE:
Take time to share lies that you can laugh with each other about (see Day #5).

IF TIME ALLOWS:
Discuss how you are doing in overcoming destination disease (Day #3).
Pray with each other.
Share other thoughts about joy.
Discuss creative ideas of how to walk in greater joy.

Possessing Joy

Week Two

"Then Jesus called a little child to Him, set him in the midst of them, and said, 'Assuredly, I say to you, <u>unless you are converted and become as little children</u>, you will by no means enter the kingdom of heaven. Therefore whoever humbles himself as this little child is the greatest in the kingdom of heaven'" (Matthew 18:2-4).

Jesus said that we must be converted (changed) and become as little children. We can learn much concerning life attitudes from watching children. There are many attributes that children have which we need to embrace (trust, simplicity, adventuresome, being a dreamer, forgiveness, love, enthusiasm, etc.).

One other characteristic of children that separates them from adults is laughter. I have read in different places that children laugh an average of 400 times a day, while adults laugh only 15 times per day. When people get older, something happens which decreases laughter (and I propose to you that this "something" is not a good thing). Laughter's decline is not rooted in faith or intimacy with God; but it comes from stress, "growing up", unbelief and religious tradition.

I suggest we make it our goal to laugh 400 times a day. It may take us years to reach that level, but at least we will know what our goal is. Some would say such an ambition is ludicrous and unimportant in the big picture of Christian living. I would disagree and say that laughter should be a regular discipline because it will enhance our longevity, health, mental well-being and strength. Hmm, maybe a merry heart is indeed good medicine; and maybe being <u>converted</u> to increasing laughter is a part of what Jesus meant in Matthew 18:2-4. What do you think?

Declare: I am becoming more like a little child every day. I live in a wonderful world of new adventures and big dreams. I also laugh as little children laugh. I regularly chuckle, giggle, snicker, hoot, snort, guffaw*, chortle**, have hysterics and double-up in hilarity.

* guffaw – a loud and raucous laugh
** chortle – a noisy, gleeful laugh

Clean Out Your Pipes

Have you ever tasted water that runs through rusty pipes? You are expecting to be refreshed, but there is a taste and after-taste that makes the water less than pleasant to drink. The water is tainted by the vessel it is flowing through. It may be great water, but you would never know it because the channel it went through has polluted it.

In a similar way, truth that flows through unclean "pipes" is harder to receive. This happens when teaching or revelation comes through a life that is stuck in frustration, fear, bitterness, anger, a bad God concept or personal hopelessness. These pipes are a person's <u>life attitudes</u> that affect the purity of the truth presented. The lack of hope and empowering grace are the main symptoms of pipes that need to be cleaned. It should be every person's desire to be a clean pipeline for God*.

How then can we keep our pipes untainted so that hope and grace are attached to everything we say? One of the ways is to laugh a lot. Laughter has an amazing way of taking the "spirit of heaviness" off of our lives (Isaiah 61:3). Godly humor gives us a new perspective that helps us to see reality rather than the falsehood that supports our unhappiness. Our inner trouble is greatly associated with the way we think, and humor can change the way we think. <u>We need to understand that it is not the situation that creates our distress, but it is the conclusions that we place on those situations</u>. Humor adjusts the meaning of our circumstances so that they are not so overwhelming (and so that we can begin to focus on God's promises instead of the problem). So let's use regular laughter as a cleansing agent to our spiritual pipes. We (and others) will be glad we did.

Declare: Hope, love and grace are attached to everything I say (even when I have to say difficult things). I have pipes that are not tainted or plugged, but they are regularly cleansed through hearty laughter. The joy of the Lord is not only strength to me, but to others through me.

* It is important to know that a "bad taste" concerning what we hear may result from our own unresolved issues and not just those of the speaker.

DAY #10 *Serve the Lord With Gladness (And With Enthusiasm)*

"Make a joyful shout to the LORD, all you lands! <u>Serve the LORD with gladness</u>; come before His presence with singing" (Psalm 100:1-2). This is an amazing portion of Scripture that instructs us to live a life of celebration and joy in our serving Jesus. It is a powerful encouragement and command that neutralizes grumbling.

"<u>Gladly serving" is a catalytic mindset that provides a secret door to our prophetic destiny</u>. On the surface it might not seem that significant, but it is. Whenever we consistently relinquish joy in an assignment from God, we have most likely hit the ceiling of our ministry influence. Our gladness level is one indicator of whether we are ready for greater responsibilities and callings.

We are called to minister in faith and love. These qualities are positive forces that generate enthusiasm – which is foundational for gladness. Enthusiasm first appeared in English in 1603 with the meaning "possession by a god." The source of the word is the Greek *enthousiasmos*, which ultimately comes from the adjective *entheos*, "having the god within."

Gladness and enthusiasm are spiritual "muscles" that can be developed to higher levels because they are already resident in us. (The God of the universe is both enthusiastic and glad – and He wants to be released through us in all we do.) If we have the habit of "serving the Lord with grumbling" or without passion, then it may take a while to radically increase joy in ministry (but the effort and journey are worth it).

Here is a key to help you: <u>Act more glad and enthusiastic than you really feel</u>. As you do so, you will find that your emotions will catch up to your actions. Then your "muscles" of gladness and enthusiasm will grow, and you will increase your influence for Christ (because you have overcome the lies that robbed you of serving our Lord in faith with joy.)

Declare: I serve the Lord with gladness. I am enthusiastic about the opportunities to minister in the name of Jesus. <u>I am an increasing joy</u> to those who are around me.

"For as the heavens are higher than the earth, so are My ways higher than your ways, and My thoughts than your thoughts" (Isaiah 55:9). God's ways are very different than our ways and must be intentionally pursued. "Do not be conformed to this world, but be transformed by the renewing of your mind" . . . (Romans 12:2).

Proverbs 13:15 states that "the way of the unfaithful is hard." If you want long-term unhappiness, then do it your way. Do you want long-term joy? Then, do it God's way.

Let's imagine that you ask two people to stand before you. The first has served Jesus all his life with true love, humility, faith and following the ways of God. The second has served the devil from his youth. He has done it his way in regards to relationships, choices, money, sex, attitudes and other areas. How do you think these two would compare? It would be obvious that God's ways are a blessing and our ways lead to a curse.

There is "pleasure in sin <u>for a season</u>" (Hebrews 11:25). It may appear that God's people are missing out on the "fun" of the world; but deep joy comes through healthy relationships, godly attitudes, wise choices and an eternal perspective. God's joy will far exceed any temporary thrill that comes from doing it our own way. (We are like a car that runs best when the owner's manual is followed. It's dumb to ignore the red light on the dashboard!)

So, do we do it our way or God's way? Do we build on the rock or on the sand (Matthew 7:24-27)? The quality of our lives and the quality of our emotions are influenced dramatically by our choices in life. It is the wise person who puts off temporary pleasure for lasting and eternal joy. Jesus "endured the cross for the joy that was set before Him" (Hebrews 12:2). We may have to experience short-term "suffering" (I Peter 4:1) by committing to purity, honesty, the marriage covenant, forgiveness, ministry to others and obeying God; but the reward will be great for us (and our descendents). Truly, God's ways are indescribably good.

Declare: I love God's ways. I build my life on the rock of God's word. I obey God, and my joy is full as a result.

DAY #12 *The Foreboding Spirit*
(Murphy's Law)

" . . . put off . . . your former conduct . . . and be renewed in the spirit of your mind . . . that you put on the new man which was created according to God, in true righteousness and holiness" (Ephesians 4:22-24).

This passage speaks of the "spirit of your mind." I believe this is the subconscious part of us that is the driving force of our attitudes and actions. These are strongholds (both positive and negative) that have been established through repeated thoughts and words (Romans 10:17). As we pursue "full joy", it is important to know that unchallenged lying thoughts will create and maintain strongholds of the enemy in the spirit of our minds (2 Cor. 10:3-5).

Many have a stronghold of foreboding, which is having a feeling that something bad is going to happen. Those who have this attitude will not experience much joy. It is the opposite of hope and faith. It is "the confident expectation that bad is coming." Those plagued with this are regularly bracing themselves to "have the rug pulled out from under them again."

Murphy's Law seems to be a major pipeline for foreboding. Who was Murphy anyway? His mantra is "whatever can go wrong, will go wrong. If the toast falls on the floor, it will always fall butter side down; or the wind will always blow in the direction of the non-smoker, etc." Murphy's philosophy is "smile, tomorrow will be worse." Obviously, there is a lot of "tongue in cheek" humor with this, but many unconsciously believe these "laws." This belief, un-fortunately, attracts problems to them and thus reinforce the lies.

We can demolish the foreboding spirit stronghold by:
confessing it as a sin (1 John 1:9)
proactively declaring truth that will build positive expectancy (faith) in our lives (Romans 4:17)
feeding on the materials of faith teachers (Romans 10:17)
becoming accountable for our thoughts (1 John 1:7)
persevering in changing our thinking because our experience will catch up to our beliefs (Matthew 9:29)
laughing when the devil says foreboding lies to us (Ps 2:1-4)

Declare: I reject foreboding and embrace hope and joy. I am now building a stronghold of joy in my life.

> *The art of being happy lies in the power of extracting happiness from common things.* — *Henry Ward Beecher*

Health Benefits of Laughter

In 2001 there were two studies that showed that a "good laugh" can strengthen your immune system. In one, which was published in the <u>Journal of the American Medical Association,</u> scientists exposed 26 people to allergens which produced allergy symptoms and then let them view a 90-minute Charlie Chaplin film. The allergy symptoms were reduced in all 26 subjects for four hours after the video. The other study, published in <u>Alternative Therapies in Health and Medicine,</u> looked for an increase in immune function through laughter. 52 healthy men watched an hour-long comedy video. They were measured before, during, and after the video for immunity markers like their T cell counts. It was discovered that just one hour of laughter boosted their immune function for up to 12 hours. Experts say that stress reduction seems to be the key for a stronger immune system, and even a few hearty chuckles a day can do wonders to lower stress. These studies support the belief that laughter can be a good antibiotic and humor can help fight germs.

Something to laugh about (another pun)

Mahatma Gandhi, as you know, walked barefoot most of the time, which produced an impressive set of calluses on his feet. He also ate very little, which made him rather frail and, with his odd diet, he suffered from bad breath. This made him a super calloused fragile mystic hexed by halitosis.

> *And these things we write to*
> *you that your joy be full.*
> I John 1:4

THE FIVE DEVOTIONALS FROM THIS PAST WEEK
400 Laughs a Day
Clean Out Your Pipes
Serve the Lord With Gladness & Enthusiasm
God's Way is the High Way
The Foreboding Spirit (Murphy's Law)

TWO ACTIONS TO TAKE:
Read or review each of the week's five devotionals.
Read out loud each of the five declarations at the end of the devotionals.

FOUR QUESTIONS TO ASK:
Which of the five devotionals spoke to you in the greatest way? Why?
What one sentence from the five devotionals stood out to you the most? Why did this speak to you?
How did you do with last week's steps to increase your strength through joy?
What two or three steps can you take this week to move forward in strengthening your life through joy?

FURTHER ACTIONS TO TAKE:
Take time to share lies that you can laugh with each other about (see Day #5).

IF TIME ALLOWS:
Pray with each other.
Share other thoughts about joy.
Discuss creative ideas of how to walk in greater joy.

Possessing Joy

Week Three

DAY #15 *The Joy of the Lord is Your Strength*

In Nehemiah 10, Ezra and others read aloud the Book of the Law of Moses. This occurred after the rebuilding of the walls of Jerusalem. It was a very emotional time for those listening, and they started to weep. Nehemiah said, " . . . this day is holy to our Lord. Do not sorrow, <u>for the joy of the LORD is your strength</u>" (Nehemiah 8:10).

Samson had a secret to his strength. It was found in the events surrounding his birth and the Nazarite vow he took (which was confirmed by not cutting his hair). It gave him a decisive advantage in life by having supernatural strength. People were astonished at what he could do.

Do we have a secret to our strength? Is there something that gives us unusual vigor and power? Is there something we can tap into that helps move us from "strength to strength"?

Listen to this: "Blessed is the man whose <u>strength</u> is in You, whose heart is set on pilgrimage. As they pass through the Valley of Baca, <u>they make it a spring</u>; the rain also covers it with pools. They go from <u>strength to strength</u> . . . " (Psalm 84:5-7). The Valley of Baca is literally the "valley of weeping." A pilgrimage is a journey to a holy place. <u>Supernatural strength will increase to those who move forward on a pilgrimage to transform hopelessness into places of life and joy.</u> This life-attitude of turning our problem into our opportunity will cause us to find strength, and then move us from "strength to strength" in ways that will amaze others and ourselves.

Let's practice joy. We can start by asking God for a revelation of the truth that the greatest thing we need is a new way of looking at life. Pray this with me: "Jesus, I ask you to cause me to see Your goodness and Your promises like never before. Help me to celebrate these, even in my Valley of Baca."

Declare: The joy of the Lord is my strength. I am increasing in joy daily. It is a secret in my life for endurance and power (spiritual strength). I am going from strength to strength in my life.

We had a yellow lab when we lived in Nevada. Snoopy loved to eat (it showed!), and he enjoyed sleeping seemingly 22 hours a day. Even so, there was one thing we had to be careful about, or else this apathetic pooch would become hyper and start leaping with excitement. What was it? It was this: moving his leash so that it made some kind of noise.

Snoopy lived for walks, and a noisy leash was the indicator to him that something good was coming. Even if this dog was sleeping deeply (with twitching and deep snoring), the leash sound would cause him to come forth as if he was shot out of a cannon. Many times we took walks that were unplanned because we could not resist the enthusiasm we saw. Selah!

The Lord spoke to me through Snoopy's actions. "Steve, keep your eager anticipation in life. Always be listening for any sign of My 'moving.' When you hear a jangle in the Spirit, respond. Don't become old in your attitude and lose the wonder of unusual coincidences and the hearing of testimonies. Stay alive in Me."

It's vital to cultivate expectancy, or else our joy and hope will decline. (Little children at Christmas are an example of the goal for our inward life-attitudes.) And here is an amazing thing – this outlook can be cultivated as we receive new revelation of His goodness and as we learn the habit of responding to any "little" thing He may be doing.

"Now may the God of hope fill you with all joy and peace in believing, that you may abound in hope by the power of the Holy Spirit" (Romans 15:13). Hope is the positive, optimistic expectation that good is coming.

So, like Snoopy, let's always be ready to jump up and abound in the Spirit. Let's keep our ears perked for the jangle of a testimony, a soul saved, a changed life, a Bible verse shared, a healing, a miracle, a revival report, a prayer prayed, a promise given, a report of seeing angels, or any other demonstration by God.

Declare: I delight in what God is doing rather than dwell on what the devil says He is not doing. I daily hear the sound of His moving and I respond with great delight and joy.

DAY #17 *Overcoming the Elder Brother Spirit*

The story of the prodigal son in Luke 15 has not one, but two prodigals. The younger son left his father's house and participated in sinful, wild living. The older son stayed in the house, but he left his father's heart. His joyless, critical attitude reflected that he too was a prodigal who had drifted into pride and tradition.

"Now his older son was in the field. And as he came and drew near to the house, he heard music and dancing. So he called one of the servants and asked what these things meant. And he said to him, 'Your brother has come, and because he has received him safe and sound, your father has killed the fatted calf.' But he was angry and would not go in. Therefore his father came out and pleaded with him. So he answered and said to his father, 'Lo, these many years I have been serving you; I never transgressed your commandment at any time; and yet you never gave me a young goat, that I might make merry with my friends. But as soon as this son of yours came, who has devoured your livelihood with harlots, you killed the fatted calf for him.' And he said to him, 'Son, you are always with me, and all that I have is yours. It was right that we should make merry and be glad, for your brother was dead and is alive again, and was lost and is found'" (Luke 15:25-32).

The "elder brother spirit" can come on any of us if we are not careful. It is evidenced by: 1) being disturbed by "too much" celebration and joy in the church; 2) being jealous over the grace that others receive; 3) having a competitive spirit; 4) focusing more on performance than on relationship; 5) being bitter at God (things are unfair); and 6) being isolated and unwilling to participate with the "family."

Certainly we need mature fathers and mothers in our midst that can help us to not forget the ancient boundaries (Proverbs 23:10) of the faith and help us maintain proper biblical order; but elder brothers have the tendency to "major in minors" and to devalue the role that joy (making merry) has in our lives. Truly, the presence of joy is one of the main signs of spiritual maturity.

Declare: I am growing into a true father or mother in the Spirit. My joy is increasing as I take this journey into greater spiritual maturity.

DAY #18 *Rejoice in That Day and Leap for Joy*

Luke 6:22-23 would probably make The Top Ten List of extraordinary things Jesus said. He says, "Blessed are you when men hate you, and when they exclude you, and revile you, and cast out your name as evil, for the Son of Man's sake. Rejoice in that day and leap for joy! For indeed your reward is great in heaven, for in like manner their fathers did to the prophets."

This passage not only tells us what to do when we are persecuted for our connection to Jesus, but it reveals three powerful life principles which will dramatically impact our lives.

First, we are to intentionally stir up joy when things are tough. This is a choosing to go against negative emotions by learning how to "encourage ourselves in the Lord" (see what David did in 1 Samuel 30:6).

Secondly, we are to rejoice "in that day." Just as Ephesians 4:26 exhorts us to deal with anger and bitterness on a daily basis ("do not let the sun go down on your wrath"); we are called to not allow a day to end without rejoicing in the face of opposing feelings and circumstances.

Thirdly, Jesus said we are to "leap for joy." Wow! It is obvious that the situation Jesus describes in Luke 6 is not a time where most of us will feel like leaping, but He is giving us an important secret for life. It's this: the key to breaking off spirits of heaviness is to increase our physical demonstrativeness in proportion to the emotional attack that is coming against us. This can be done through leaping, talking loudly to our own soul (as David did in the Psalms), dancing, running, shouting or aggressively declaring God's promises.

"Rejoice in that day and leap for joy" is a compass for those who want to travel up to the headwaters of God's joy. Let's encourage each other to find the hidden truths of Luke 6:23.

Declare: I am receiving great revelation about rejoicing in the Lord. I am choosing to rejoice sooner (than I used to) when tough things happen. I am learning to rejoice and leap for joy on the same day the challenge comes. I am on a glorious journey toward full joy.

Enemy of Joy: A Critical Spirit

An obsessive attitude of disapproval and finding fault is called a "critical spirit." Those with this attitude regularly see negatives, regularly complain and are usually upset with something or someone. Their identity is rooted in what they are against rather than what they are for. This spirit greatly hinders joy.

A critical spirit is fueled by insecurity, competition, perfectionism and self-criticism. Insecurity causes us to focus on the faults of others so that we don't have to fully face our own issues. (We tend to judge ourselves by our motives and others by their actions.) Competition creates an "us against them" mentality. (The successes of others are seen as a threat to our own future.) Perfectionism makes us "not fun to be with" because we give little encouragement for improvements or positive steps made by others. The biggie, though, is self-criticism. This greatly feeds the critical spirit. Let's explore this one further.

When Jesus said, "Love your neighbor as yourself" (Matthew 22:39), He was giving us more than a command. He was sharing this principle of life: how we feel about ourselves will strongly affect how we feel about others. If we love ourselves, we will love others. If we hate ourselves, we will have a tendency to hate others. If we accept ourselves, we will accept others. If we are critical of ourselves, we will often have a critical spirit concerning others.

Letting go of the critical spirit can be scary. There is a fear that doing this will actually increase negative behavior in others. (It is believed that keeping negative will help others "tow the line.") The use of criticism as a motivational tool may bring some short-term positive results, but it will produce long-term relationship strain (as well as damage the "father concept" in people's lives.)

When we get a life-altering revelation of how much we are loved and forgiven, then we are on the road to eliminating the critical spirit. When we see how much mercy we have been given, then we will give mercy. Of course, this does not mean that we are ignoring problems that need to be addressed; but we will do so from a spirit of love and wholeness, and not from a "critical spirit."

Declare: I have great joy because I am loved and forgiven by God. I see the good in others. The critical spirit is far from me.

When was the last time you laughed for the sheer joy of your salvation? People are not attracted to somber doctrines. There is no persuasive power in a gloomy and morbid religion. Let the world see your joy and you won't be able to keep them away. To be filled with God is to be filled with joy. -
Anonymous

Health Benefits of Laughter

A study by cardiologists at the University of Maryland Medical Center in Baltimore gives evidence that laughter, along with an active sense of humor, helps protect against a heart attack. The study, which was the first to indicate that laughter may help prevent heart disease, found that people with heart disease were 40 percent less likely to laugh in a variety of situations compared to people of the same age without heart disease. The results of the study were presented at the Scientific Session of the American College of Cardiology on March 7, 2005, in Orlando, Florida.

Something to laugh about

A church secretary takes a call. The caller says, "Is the head hog at the trough there?"

The secretary says, "Please Sir, do not refer to our pastor as the head hog at the trough. That is very insulting."

"Oh, I'm very sorry. I meant nothing by that. It's just a local phrase we use in the part of the country I come from. The real reason I called was to donate $50,000.00 to your building fund."

The secretary says, "Hold on. I see the 'Big Oinker' coming through the door right now."

...Whom having not seen you love. Though now
you do not see Him, yet believing, you rejoice
with joy inexpressible and full of glory...
I Peter 1:8

THE FIVE DEVOTIONALS FROM THIS PAST WEEK
The Joy of the Lord is Your Strength
Eager Anticipation
Overcoming the Elder Brother Spirit
Rejoice in That Day and Leap for Joy
Enemy of Joy: A Critical Spirit

TWO ACTIONS TO TAKE:
Read or review each of the week's five devotionals.
Read out loud each of the five declarations at the end of the devotionals.

FOUR QUESTIONS TO ASK:
Which of the five devotionals spoke to you in the greatest way? Why?
What one sentence from the five devotionals stood out to you the most? Why did this speak to you?
How did you do with last week's steps to increase your strength through joy?
What two or three steps can you take this week to move forward in strengthening your life through joy?

FURTHER ACTIONS TO TAKE:
Take time to share lies that you can laugh with each other about (see Day #5).

IF TIME ALLOWS:
Discuss how you are doing in overcoming destination disease (Day #3).
Pray with each other.
Share other thoughts about joy.
Discuss creative ideas of how to walk in greater joy.

Possessing Joy

Week Four

DAY #22 *The Angel's Announcement About Jesus*

I don't completely understand how it works when an angel gets an assignment to give a message to humans, but I am sure that the words are chosen very carefully to convey the highest purposes of God. With that in mind, the angel's announcement to the shepherds about the birth of Jesus would therefore be quite instructive to. "Then the angel said to them, 'Do not be afraid, for behold, I bring you good tidings of great joy which will be to all people. For there is born to you this day in the city of David a Savior, who is Christ the Lord'" (Luke 2:8-11).

"Good tidings of great joy" is the first thing that is said in the angelic announcement. Let that sink in for a moment. The angel did not say, "I bring you news of a teaching that I hope you can follow"; or "I bring you news that Jesus is coming; and, boy, is He mad!" No, the message was, "It's time to celebrate! God is doing what you couldn't. He is making a way where there was no way. You are being saved from the curse, rejection, shame, punishment, poverty and sickness; and from performance-based living. The door is being opened to eternal life, intimacy with the Father, the indwelling of the Holy Spirit and so much more. It is incredible, joyous news!"

What is the first thing that people hear from the church? Is it a message of good news or is it a message that is bad news (because it focuses more on what we need to do rather than on what Jesus has already done)? Churches that rejoice continually in God's goodness will attract people who need hope and are often the castaways of religious churches that have a tendency to block grace by legalism and emphasizing the works of the law.

The angel knew something that we must know. If we don't believe we have fantastic news to share, then we need to ask God to open our eyes to the greatness of our salvation. And, you know what? He will!

Declare: I join the angels in declaring good tidings of great joy. I am receiving an increasing revelation of God that makes me want to participate in outrageous celebration. The message of Jesus is good news!

DAY #23 *Right Song, Wrong Side (The Sacrifice of Joy)*

People of joy learn to rejoice in God's promises even before they have experienced the victory. Their gladness is not linked to circumstances, but it is rooted in trust in God.

There was a remarkable praise service that is recorded in Exodus 15 after the children of Israel's miraculous deliverance from Egypt through the Red Sea. "Then Moses and the children of Israel sang this song <u>to the LORD</u> . . . : 'I will sing to the LORD, for He has triumphed gloriously! The horse and its rider He has thrown into the sea!' . . . Then Miriam . . . and all the women went out after her with timbrels and with dances. And Miriam answered them: 'Sing to the LORD, For He has triumphed gloriously!'" (Exodus 15:1,20,21).

Listen however to what had happened before these miracles. " . . . the children of Israel lifted their eyes, and behold, the Egyptians marched after them. So they were very afraid . . . Then they said to Moses, 'Because there were no graves in Egypt, have you taken us away to <u>die in the wilderness</u>? . . . Is this not the word that we told you in Egypt, saying, 'Let us alone that we may serve the Egyptians? For it would have been better for us to serve the Egyptians than that we should die in the wilderness'" (Exodus 14:10-12). It was not a pretty picture.

The merriment in chapter 15 was not wrong. Surely we need to celebrate radically after victories. Here though is the problem: they had the right song (praise), but it was on the wrong side of the Red Sea. They were out of Egypt, but Egypt was still firmly in them. Their grumbling was actually a bigger problem than the problem of the sea and the Egyptians.

What is the point of all this? Hear this: "And now my head shall be lifted up above my enemies all around me; Therefore, <u>I will offer sacrifices of joy</u> in His tabernacle; I will sing, yes, I will sing praises to the LORD" (Psalm 27:6). <u>One key for our lives is to intentionally stir up joy before we see the victory.</u> It is called "the sacrifice of joy." Let's proactively give this sacrifice.

Declare: I celebrate now. I rejoice now. I dance now. I declare the victory now. I don't wait for the sea to part, but I offer the sacrifice of praise – that is, the fruit of my lips, giving thanks to His name (see Hebrews 13:15).

I remember the tent ministry well. It came to the town where I was a pastor in rural Nevada. I had agreed to help sponsor them for their ten days in our community. I had my concerns, but I still said yes.

You see, this was a special "renewal tent" that had wild things happen in it. (I had heard of its reputation!) I had partially experienced some of these types of things; so I was both excited (I wanted more of God) and nervous (what if it, or I, got out of control).

When I saw the tent, I saw a flag flying over it saying, "The Party is Here." This phrase troubled me. I was not comfortable with a church ministry saying this. It did not seem right. What would people think?

Well, ten days later my thoughts had changed. We had two meetings a day and I experienced God in powerful ways. His presence increased throughout the week. People were responding in different ways. Some shook, some fell under the power of God, some laughed uncontrollably, and many were so full of the Spirit that they acted like they were drunk. It truly became a big party. Yes, the party was there and those attending did not want to leave. There was child-like hilarity. There was deep relational bonding. There was a great love for Jesus that infected our lives.

My attitude changed during these meetings. I realized that religious tradition had made me stuffy and unable to <u>cut loose in God</u>. I was bound in many ways to a spirit of control and a fear of embarrassment. Since that time, I have concluded that each of us needs Holy Spirit "drinking buddies" who love to frolic in the presence of God. Obviously, we cannot do this at every church meeting, but what a blessing to have times to "party" in Jesus where we can laugh and be overwhelmed by His Spirit. Surprisingly, I believe it is part of the new wineskin for the days ahead (Mark 2:22).

Declare: There was a party when the Prodigal Son came home (Luke 15); and, now, I have come home knowing it is proper to party in Jesus now. I am serious about God and the kingdom, but I run to the party because it is part of experiencing the full joy that Jesus has for me.

DAY #25 *God Loves a Hilarious Giver*

It would be good for us to perk up our ears when God says he loves something. One of those times is found in 2 Corinthians 9. "But this I say: He who sows sparingly will also reap sparingly, and he who sows bountifully will also reap bountifully. So let each one give as he purposes in his heart, not grudgingly or of necessity; <u>for God loves a cheerful giver</u>" (2 Corinthians 9:6,7).

This word "cheerful" is a great word. It means happy and optimistic. From the context, we can see that we are to give happily, and with optimism, because we realize that we are participating in the wonderful spiritual phenomena of giving.

We can take this further by understanding that the Greek word for cheerful is hilaros. Can you see something here? <u>Hilarious</u> comes from "hilaros." This understanding takes our attitude about giving to another level. It is one thing to be happy and optimistic as we give, but it is quite another to be hilarious in our giving. Optimism is the reflection of a prosperous soul (3 John 2); but regular, hilarious giving reveals that we have established radical core values that will accelerate the removal of limits and constraints from our lives. It is to this type of person that the Bible says, "God loves." Of course, God loves everyone, but there is something that touches His heart when He sees a person become a joyous giver.

We are told to not give "grudgingly" (2 Corinthians 9:7). This would mean that we are doing so with "sorrow, pain, grief, annoyance, affliction, and mourning." If hilarious giving attracts God to us, then "annoyed giving" would seem to create a distance between His empowering grace and us. <u>Our attitude about giving indeed becomes a thermostat that will set the "temperature" for our Christian experience and the quality of our lives</u>. If hilarious giving is something that God loves, then we need to overcome stinginess in our soul and intentionally develop this abounding cheerfulness. It is a journey that will take us from glory to glory, strength to strength and joy to joy.

Declare: I am a cheerful giver. I am becoming a hilarious giver who jumps for joy when I get to give. It is something that God loves and I love it, too.

DAY #26 *Enemy of Joy:*
Excessive Introspection

Here is a truth to remember: negative, excessive introspection leads to discouragement and ultimately to depression. When we constantly try to find out what is wrong with us, we will be on a journey that leads to the Christian wilderness. Certainly, we cannot be in denial about negative tendencies in our lives, but the way to overcome these is not by continual self-analysis. This kind of introspection can be a major enemy of joy for our lives.

Excessive introspection is the detailed, mental self-examination of feelings, thoughts and motives. It is the fruit of the works of the law and performance Christianity. The book of Galatians repudiates this as not only unbiblical, but completely counterproductive (Gal. 5:1-6). Listen to what Paul says. "O foolish Galatians! . . . Did you receive the Spirit by the works of the law, or by the hearing of faith? Are you so foolish? <u>Having begun in the Spirit, are you now being made perfect by the flesh</u>? . . . Therefore He who supplies the Spirit to you and works miracles among you, does He do it by the works of the law, or by the hearing of faith?" (Galatians 3:1-5). Introspection and works are not the keys to miracles, Christian maturity or the supply of the Spirit. It is "the hearing of faith."

Paul adds in chapter five, "I say then: <u>Walk in the Spirit, and you shall not fulfill the lust of the flesh</u>" (Galatians 5:16). We are told to activate the positive ("walk in the Spirit") and then the negative ("lust of the flesh") won't happen. <u>The key to getting rid of darkness is to turn the light on, not to continually analyze the various aspects of the darkness</u>.

In conclusion, it is important to deal with our weaknesses primarily by growing in faith and filling our lives with the things of the Spirit. Certainly, we need accountability and responsibility for these weaknesses, but this must be done as part of a bigger plan that primarily includes "mega doses" of God's Word and Spirit. Excessive Introspection won't help this plan, so stay away from it.

Declare: I reject excessive, negative introspection as a means to Christian maturity. I walk in the Spirit and do not fulfill the lusts of the flesh. The "hearing of faith" is alive in me and causes me to mature, have an increasing supply of the Spirit and have miracles work through me.

True happiness is not attained through self-gratification, but through fidelity to a worthy purpose. - Helen Keller

Health Benefits of Laughter:

The Science of Laughter Discovery Health website reports that when we laugh, natural killer cells that destroy tumors and viruses increase in our bodies. Also increasing are Gamma-interferon (a disease-fighting protein), T-cells (important for our immune system) and B-cells (which make disease-fighting antibodies). This website also states that laughter lowers blood pressure and increases oxygen in the blood, which promotes health and healing.

Something to Laugh About

A man walks into a restaurant and sits down next to a man with a dog at his feet. "Does your dog bite?"

"No."

A few minutes later the dog takes a huge chunk out of his leg.

"I thought you said your dog didn't bite!" the man says indignantly.

"That's not my dog."

Let all those who seek You rejoice and be glad in You; Let such as love Your salvation say continually, "The LORD be magnified!"
Psalm 40:16

THE FIVE DEVOTIONALS FROM THIS PAST WEEK

The Angel's Announcement About Jesus
Right Song, Wrong Side (The Sacrifice of Joy)
The Party is Here
God Loves a Hilarious Giver
Enemy of Joy: Excessive Introspection

TWO ACTIONS TO TAKE:

Read or review each of the week's five devotionals.
Read out loud each of the five declarations at the end of the devotionals.

FOUR QUESTIONS TO ASK:

Which of the five devotionals spoke to you in the greatest way? Why?
What one sentence from the five devotionals stood out to you the most? Why did this speak to you?
How did you do with last week's steps to increase your strength through joy?
What two or three steps can you take this week to move forward in strengthening your life through joy?

FURTHER ACTIONS TO TAKE:

Take time to share lies that you can laugh with each other about (see Day #5).

IF TIME ALLOWS:

Discuss how you are doing in overcoming destination disease (Day #3).
Pray with each other.
Share other thoughts about joy.
Discuss creative ideas of how to walk in greater joy.

Possessing Joy

Week Five

"Now may the God of hope fill you with all joy and peace in believing, that you may abound in hope by the power of the Holy Spirit" (Romans 15:13). This is one of my favorite Bible verses. Its reference to hope is foundational for those who are on the "joy journey." Remember, hope is the "confident, optimistic expectation that good is coming." It is the "soil" that faith and joy must have their roots in.

Paul prays that the Roman people will be "filled" with ALL joy. Concerning this joy let me ask you: is joy an emotion or a substance? It is an emotion, but it is primarily a substance – something that can be imparted and something that we can defeat the enemy with. The apostle prayed that we would be filled with it. This would seem to indicate that we could also be empty of it, half-filled or have other levels of joy. Is there a kind of "spiritual dip stick" that measures our joy level? I wonder.

What strikes me more though in this verse is the phrase "in believing." It says, "Now may the God of hope fill you with all joy and peace in believing." Our joy and other emotions result mostly from what we believe. This verse implies that believing our God is the God of hope is a key to experiencing joy and peace. This hope is based on the finished work of Christ, His love, His goodness and His promises. As we replace the lies of the devil with truth (John 8:31,32), we will see a corresponding increase in our joy level. We will indeed be filled with all joy.

Romans 15:13 starts with the word now. It does not say tomorrow, or next week or next year. It says now! It does not give us the idea that we will be filled when our circumstances change. No, it says, "believe now and you will be filled." Let's receive a filling of joy and peace by faith right now.

Declare: The God of hope is continually filling me with joy. I am a believing believer who believes in His goodness and promises. I am being filled more and more as a result. Right now I choose to walk in an abounding hope that will ignite my joy like never before.

For the Joy Set Before Him

"Looking unto Jesus, the author and finisher of our faith, who for the joy that was set before Him endured the cross, despising the shame, and has sat down at the right hand of the throne of God" (Hebrews 12:2).

One of the ways to possess and keep joy is to be able to "see through" the challenges of life and focus on the joy that is set before us. There are two specific joys that we can fix our gaze upon that will propel greater joy now.

First, we can focus on the joy of our heavenly reward. We are saved by faith (not our goodness); but we can "lay up treasures in heaven" (Matthew 6:20) that will have benefits now and for eternity. Some Christians are too earthly minded to be any heavenly good. (I hope my corny humor caused a chuckle or two.) Listen, our journey here on earth is but a moment in our eternal life as Christians. What we believe and do in Jesus' name will lay a good foundation for this life and the life to come. This realization can bring a joyous perspective to our time here on earth.

Secondly, we understand that vision for the future brings strength and joy for the present. Consider an athlete who has an ambition to achieve a great goal. This dream (future joy) causes an increase in enthusiasm to overcome challenges and in establishing consistency in daily "life-launching" habits. Where there is no vision for the future, there can be little power or joy for the present.

Jesus endured the ultimate negative circumstance (the cross) by focusing on the joy that was set before him. He has set an example for us. He is the author and the finisher of our faith. He will help us walk in joy-filled faith by causing us to keep our eyes on the greater joy ahead.

Declare: I am empowered to face my present with faith because I have a great joy set before me. This future joy causes me to persevere through tough times with joy now. I am a person with great vision for this life. I also rejoice as I consider heaven and its reward.

Rejoice in the Lord Always

"Rejoice in the Lord always. Again I will say, rejoice! Let your gentleness be known to all men. The Lord is at hand. Be anxious for nothing, but in everything by prayer and supplication, with thanksgiving, let your requests be made known to God; and the peace of God, which surpasses all understanding, will guard your hearts and minds through Christ Jesus" (Philippians 4:4-7).

Paul is writing to the Philippians from jail. One of the main themes of this New Testament book is joy. He emphasizes this when he says, "Rejoice in the Lord always." He not only says it once; but he repeats it, just in case we somehow overlook its significance.

This command is in three parts. First, we are to rejoice. This means to be glad and to take delight. Secondly, we are to rejoice in the Lord. We are not to just think positively, but we are to "re-joy" by exulting in the various aspects of our Lord's nature and promises concerning what we are tempted to worry about. Lastly, we are to rejoice always. It is to be a continual expression of our lives (not just something we do in church or when we feel like it). Remember, this is not a suggestion, but it's a command. That may depress some, but it excites me because God never commands us to do something He has not already empowered us to be able to perform. Yippee! Now that is something to rejoice about!

There is one more thing to see here before we close. The verses that follow "rejoice in the Lord always" tell us to absolutely and totally reject worry. We are to empty ourselves of this crippler in our lives. This will occur as we have a revelation of truth to replace the worry with prayer, thanksgiving and rejoicing in the Lord. Thankful rejoicing is truly a key for a powerful prayer life and to walking in deep peace and joy.

Declare: I am learning how to rejoice in the Lord always. I continually turn my heart toward his goodness, love and promises. I verbalize praise, thanksgiving and adoration to Jesus. I don't wait for circumstances to change before rejoicing, but my rejoicing changes circumstances.

There are many important disciplines to develop in life. It is the wise person who establishes regular non-negotiable "customs" like Daniel (see Daniel 6:10). The quality of our life is impacted greatly by the development of consistency in areas such as time with God, Bible reading, fellowship, positive declaration, thankfulness, etc. If we proactively put these in our schedule, we will set ourselves up for success in our Christian life.

One non-negotiable custom that is often overlooked is joy and laughter. "A merry heart is good like a medicine" (Proverbs 17:22). We've already acknowledged that "Dr. God" has given us a wonderful prescription for health and longevity. Now it is up to us to find a way to consistently make this happen in our lives (and not just wait for special moments to develop on their own).

Laughter clubs are appearing all over the world. (Do an Internet search on this and you will be amazed at what you find.) There are many people who participate in a laughter group one or more times a week. Even though we may not be able to join such a group, there are many ways we can increase joy and laughter. Here are some suggestions

Watch humorous, but clean, video presentations.

Become a student of animals. They are funny.

Get CD's of people laughing uncontrollably.

Create a regular joy prayer meeting where you laugh at the lies of the devil (Psalm 2:1-4).

Find Christian friends to have special joy times of stirring up joy, childlikeness and hilarity.

Look in the mirror and tell yourself this: Don't take yourself so seriously. Then laugh.

Give expression to your "inner laugh." Don't just laugh on the inside.

Laughter is like a muscle. If we have not laughed much in recent times, it may take a while to get strong in this area. Don't be discouraged. Just set your compass toward increased chuckling, and the belly laughs will be waiting in the wings to erupt from you.

Declare: I have the discipline of joy and laughter. It is one of my non-negotiable customs and disciplines.

DAY #33 *Enemy of Joy: Being Easily Offended*

Joy cannot properly co-exist in a life that is offended. If we dwell on past hurts, we empower the devil to steal our joy. We will be weighed down with "spirits of heaviness" that will create feelings of anger, self-pity, criticism and unforgiveness.

<u>Being offended</u> means we feel insulted, mistreated, snubbed, or disrespected. All of us will experience things like these. It is important to realize though that the mistreatment itself does not cause the offense, but we choose to be offended. Joy cannot survive in an atmosphere where offense is prevalent.

<u>Joy and forgiveness walk hand in hand</u>. Wherever you find people with great joy, you will find great forgiveness in their lives (that is rooted in the revelation that they have been forgiven much by God and others). We forgive not only because it is the right thing to do, but it is also a great weapon for releasing an "open heaven" over those being forgiven and over our own lives (consider Jesus on the cross and Stephen in Acts 7 – and read John 20:23).

How can we become "unoffendable"? Here are five suggestions: 1) Realize that we offend others and need forgiveness too; 2) Understand that overcoming the tendency of being offended is necessary for maturity and effective ministry; 3) Realize that our response to a situation is almost always more important than the situation itself; 4) Increase rejoicing when offense tries to control you; and 5) Get personal ministry to resolve deep hurts.

There is one more step to take in overcoming this sin of offense and bitterness. It's this: <u>do a great work for God</u>. Nehemiah, in response to his enemies' request to meet with him in the Valley of Ono, said, "I am doing a great work, so that <u>I cannot come down</u>. Why should the work cease while I leave it and go down to you?" (Nehemiah 6:1-3). Those who focus on a big vision aren't even aware of many of the wrongs done to them, and these "history makers" know that being easily offended causes a "going down" from the high place of God's purpose.

Let's purpose to rejoice always and forgive easily. As we do, God will strengthen us in amazing ways.

Declare: I am doing a great work in God. I am not easily offended. I walk in radical forgiveness. My joy helps insulate me from offense.

A genuine revival without joy in the Lord is as impossible as spring without flowers, or day-dawn without light. - Charles Spurgeon

Health Benefits of Laughter

Researchers at Loma Linda University in Loma Linda, California, and Oakcrest Health Research Institute in Yucaipa, California, discovered that a good belly laugh (or even the anticipation of laughter) has a beneficial effect on our body's hormones. They studied 32 healthy men, half of whom were instructed to view an hour-long funny video. The other half were told to sit in a room with an assortment of magazines.

Blood was drawn from each man before, during and after the experiment. The scientists discovered (even before the video clips started to play) that those chosen to watch the humorous videos had 27 percent more beta-endorphins and 87 percent more human growth hormone in their blood on average than the other group. The levels of these beneficial hormones remained high during and after the experiment.

The research, presented in San Francisco in 2006 at an American Physiological Society session, adds to previous studies that reveal that humor has healthy "side effects", such as lowering levels of two stress hormones - cortisol and epinephrine.

Researchers stated that the benefits created by laughter are similar to those produced by exercise. For example, laughing has a positive effect on the cardiovascular system. It lowers overall blood pressure levels and decreases the resting heart rate. Also, the immune system appears to get tuned up when we laugh. Maybe we should get serious about a good laugh!

Rejoice always.
I Thessalonians 5:16

THE FIVE DEVOTIONALS FROM THIS PAST WEEK
All Joy and Peace in Believing
For the Joy Set Before Him
Rejoice in the Lord Always
The Discipline of Joy and Laughter
Enemy of Joy: Being Easily Offended

TWO ACTIONS TO TAKE:
Read or review each of the week's five devotionals.
Read out loud each of the five declarations at the end of the devotionals.

FOUR QUESTIONS TO ASK:
Which of the five devotionals spoke to you in the greatest way? Why?
What one sentence from the five devotionals stood out to you the most? Why did this speak to you?
How did you do with last week's steps to increase your strength through joy?
What two or three steps can you take this week to move forward in strengthening your life through joy?

FURTHER ACTIONS TO TAKE:
Take time to share lies that you can laugh with each other about (see Day #5).

IF TIME ALLOWS:
Discuss how you are doing in overcoming destination disease (Day #3).
Pray with each other.
Share other thoughts about joy.
Discuss creative ideas of how to walk in greater joy.

Possessing Joy

Week Six

DAY #36 *Our God Concept and Our Joy Level*

Our God-concept dramatically impacts our personality. If we think God is stoic and unemotional, then we will be stoic and unemotional. If we think He is wild and unpredictable, then we will be wild and unpredictable. If we think He is angry, we will be angry. If we think He is detached, we will be detached. If we think He is full of joy, then we will be full of joy. Our upbringing and religious experience influence greatly our God-concept; and, then, ultimately our own personality traits as well.

Certainly, God has varied emotions and cannot be limited to one particular personality trait; but if we don't have revelation of His nature, we will ultimately limit our personal development and our wholeness. Hosea said, "My people are destroyed for lack of knowledge" (Hosea 4:6). Our lack of revelation concerning the character of God will cause destruction to our potential and our influence upon others.

The Bible says, "In His presence is fullness of joy" (Psalm 16:11). Our joy will increase as we move into greater realms of His presence. Yes, we realize that His presence will not always produce joy; but if we never or rarely have "fullness of joy", then we need to take serious inventory of our concept of God. It would be probable that we are under a religious deception that is hindering us from having the "joy of the Lord" become our strength.

It is safe to say that all of us need an adjustment in how we see God. It would also appear that the church of Jesus Christ needs a greater encounter with the joy of the Lord. Pray with me. "Oh God, open the eyes of my understanding to who You really are. Help me especially to see that You are emotional and that You have great joy."

Declare: I have a relationship with a great God. He is awesome in every way. He is full of joy and throws a party in heaven whenever one person comes to Him through Jesus Christ. My concept of God is transformed daily into what it should be.

"For the kingdom of God is not eating and drinking, but righteousness and peace and <u>joy in the Holy Spirit</u>" (Romans 14:17).

I believe God wants us to keep our Christian life simple. I Corinthians 13:13 is an example of this: "And now abide faith, hope, love, these three; but the greatest of these is love" (faith, hope and love are enduring qualities to primarily focus on). Jesus also gave us simple and clear priorities to live by in Mark 12:29-31: "The first of all the commandments is: ' . . . you shall love the LORD your God with all your heart, with all your soul, with all your mind, and with all your strength. This is the first commandment. And the second, like it, is this: 'You shall love your neighbor as yourself.' There is no other commandment greater than these" (loving God and loving people is true spirituality).

Romans 14:17 adds another "list" that clarifies what is really important for our lives. This chapter discusses "disputable matters" in the church (i.e. Sabbaths, foods, etc.) Paul steers the reader away from criticism and pride in these issues by saying that the kingdom is about three things: 1) <u>Righteousness</u> – the understanding that Christ has made us blameless and has given grace to empower us to make godly decisions; 2) <u>Peace</u> – the assurance in our hearts about God's nature, His promises and our authority in Him; and 3) <u>Joy</u> – the overflow of faith and intimacy with Jesus that causes celebration and radical expectancy for the future. These three result from being "in the Holy Spirit." It is fascinating that joy made this "big three list."

Romans 14:17 propels us to understand that our inner victory over unworthiness, striving, fear and joylessness is more important than whether we eat meat or not (or other similar matters). Biblical joy is vital because it causes us to deal with the lies of the devil and develop an overflowing faith in God. These things are crucial to becoming a person who has longevity in Christ and who will make a difference in kingdom advancement.

Declare: The kingdom has much to do with joy. I do not "major" in minor legalistic issues; but I am intentionally growing in righteousness, peace and joy in the Holy Spirit.

"I take pleasure in infirmities, in reproaches, in needs, in persecutions, in distresses, for Christ's sake. For when I am weak, then I am strong" (2 Corinthians 12:10). The Apostle Paul, who wrote these words, had an amazing "philosophy" concerning difficulty and personal weakness that is a key to joy in our lives.

For most of us, our weaknesses (infirmities) depress us. Our failures and lack of strength scream at us saying: "There is something wrong with you! You are not serious about God!" Paul though took pleasure (delight) in his deficiencies and difficult circumstances. He declared, ". . . when I am weak, then I am strong." He rejoiced regarding Christ's strength flowing in his weak areas.

Before we delve more into this, let's make one thing clear. Paul's "thorn in the flesh" (which is what he is talking about in this passage) cannot be interpreted in a way that creates passiveness and fatalism in our thinking. Our interpretation of Paul's thorn (and Job's affliction) will have much to do with our level of victory in life. A misinterpretation will cause a "crack" in our faith foundation that will hinder us in praying the prayer of faith and in resisting the devil. Space does not allow for teaching on this; but understand that many Christians are joyless and hopeless because of a misunderstanding of God's sovereignty (because they believe everything that happens is God's will). See my book, *Cracks in the Foundation* for a further teaching on this.

We must have a "shift" in our thinking concerning flawed areas in us and around us. Instead of endlessly dwelling on shortcomings and limitations, let's turn our eyes to God, release our faith, and rejoice in how He is working in our lives and situations. "Thank you, Jesus, that you are doing what I cannot do! I can't wait to see how you are going to change me. I delight in You today!" This stirring up of joyous faith (in the face of failure and constraints) will be a catalyst for God's strength and deliverance to manifest.

Obviously, if our weaknesses are self-destructive and/or hurting others, we need help and accountability; but we must primarily turn our hearts joyfully to God in anticipation of seeing His strength working in us and around us.

Declare: I delight in my weaknesses and limitations because I know that God will show His strength through them.

DAY #39 *Harvest Focused or Planting Focused*

A few years ago, I felt like the Lord said to me, "Steve, I want you to be more 'planting focused' than 'harvest focused.' It will be a key for greater joy and increased effectiveness in ministry." It was a word that deeply impacted my life.

Harvest focused people are regularly looking for results and fruit to determine if they are successful or in God's will. Certainly, we cannot ignore results, but they are unreliable indicators of whether we are going in the right direction. Those who base their happiness and joy on visible fruit will not be very joyful, and will have a "roller coaster" emotional experience.

"Planting focused" people have established a clear set of core values that they are convinced will bring a great harvest. They are not disturbed by negative circumstances because they know it is impossible for the harvest not to come. " . . . for whatever a man sows, that he will also reap . . . and let us not grow weary while doing good, for in due season we shall reap if we do not lose heart" (Galatians 6:7,9). Those who persistently plant in love, faith, words, generosity and in other ways will produce a harvest.

This issue is vital for those who want to walk in joy. It is also an important leadership principle. Whether we apply this truth to ministry or to life in general; the planting focused mentality will help eliminate the tendency to speak word curses over seeds we have planted, and it will increase the "watering" of those same seeds. It will also help break the common habit of withdrawing faith just because the desired harvest was not seen.

If we have a plan from God in planting and watering, we can put up with a lot of lack and unresolved situations. On the contrary, we will be "open season" for the devil if we are using fruit and results as the main indicator of whether we are in God's will or are spiritually "successful." Indeed, our joy is greatly impacted by whether we are harvest focused or planting focused.

Declare: I set the course of my life to plant and water seeds that will bring a great harvest. I am not discouraged by negative circumstances, but I rejoice more and more in the increasing harvest that is coming.

Enemy of Joy: Victim Mentality

The "victim mentality" is when we blame others (including God) for what happens in our world. If we didn't get the promotion, it is because our boss is out to get us (not because we have a poor work ethic). If we are disrespectful or unloving, it is because life is too hard or we're too tired (not because we have chosen to be irresponsible). Victims think it is everyone else's fault. "It is not fair," they protest. The very essence of being a victim is unhappiness, not joy.

There is an intriguing story in John 5. Jesus comes to the pool of Bethesda where people were healed when the water stirred. "Now a certain man was there who had an infirmity thirty-eight years. When Jesus saw him lying there . . . He said to him, '<u>Do you want to be made well</u>?' The sick man answered Him, 'Sir, I have no man to put me into the pool when the water is stirred up; but while I am coming, another steps down before me.' Jesus said to him, 'Rise, take up your bed and walk.' And immediately the man was made well . . . " (John 5:5-9).

The question "Do you want to be made well?" is powerful. I believe it speaks of the victim mentality. This man said he was not healed because of negative circumstances against him. Jesus did not acknowledge this conclusion, but basically told him, "Stop seeing yourself as a victim and do what you think you cannot do." When he did, everything changed.

All of us have to answer the question, "Do you want to made well?" It goes to the heart of whether we will stop identifying ourselves as a victim. When we stop making excuses, we are ready for rapid growth and change. We will become honoring, loving, honest, hard working and respectful. On the surface, this sounds very "unjoyful", but nothing could be further from the truth (because it is those who believe they are a victim that are usually hopeless and unhappy). When we believe we can do something, we are empowered. And that is extremely good and joyful news.

Declare: I am not a victim. I am putting my excuses aside. I am being made well. I have hope. I am becoming responsible, honoring and loving. I am joyful now.

Joy is a net of love by which you can catch souls. A joyful heart is the inevitable result of a heart burning with love. - Mother Theresa

Health Benefits of Laughter

Laughter helps remove the negative effects of stress, which is thought to be the number one cause of death today. In researching the effects of stress on health, I have discovered that it is estimated that up to 70% of illnesses are connected to stress. Some of the health problems caused by stress are high blood pressure, heart disease, anxiety disorders, depression, frequent coughs & colds, peptic ulcers, insomnia, allergies, asthma, menstrual difficulties, tension headaches, stomach upsets and even cancer.

Frequent hearty laughter not only lowers stress, but it also helps to improve the immune system, which is a key factor in maintaining good health. Finally, laughter works out our facial muscles which can lead to a younger, healthier appearance.

Something to Laugh About

A woman went into her kitchen to find a burglar loaded down with a bunch of stuff he was stealing from her kitchen. Not having any kind of weapon to scare him off, she raised her hand and said "Acts 2:38," and proceeded to quote scripture.

The burglar froze in place and didn't move. The woman called 911, the police arrived and were amazed to find the burglar still frozen where he stood.

"What did you say to him that kept him from moving?" they asked the woman.

She told them that she had simply said Acts 2:38 and quoted scripture.

The police chuckled and escorted the burglar out to the patrol car. "Why did the woman's quoting scripture scare you so much?" they asked.

"Scripture?" said the burglar, "I thought she said she had an ax and two 38's!"

THE FIVE DEVOTIONALS FROM THIS PAST WEEK

Our God Concept and Our Joy Level
Joy is 1/3 of the Kingdom
Delighting in Weaknesses
Harvest Focused or Planting Focused
Enemy of Joy: Victim Mentality

TWO ACTIONS TO TAKE:

Read or review each of the week's five devotionals.
Read out loud each of the five declarations at the end of the devotionals.

FOUR QUESTIONS TO ASK:

Which of the five devotionals spoke to you in the greatest way? Why?
What one sentence from the five devotionals stood out to you the most? Why did this speak to you?
How did you do with last week's steps to increase your strength through joy?
What two or three steps can you take this week to move forward in strengthening your life through joy?

FURTHER ACTIONS TO TAKE:

Take time to share lies that you can laugh with each other about (see Day #5).

IF TIME ALLOWS:

Discuss how you are doing in overcoming destination disease (Day #3).
Pray with each other.
Share other thoughts about joy.
Discuss creative ideas of how to walk in greater joy.

Possessing Joy

Week Seven

"Trust in the LORD, and do good; dwell in the land, and feed on His faithfulness. <u>Delight yourself also in the LORD</u>, and He shall give you the desires of your heart" (Psalm 34:3,4). "Delight" means 1) "to gain great enjoyment or pleasure about something"; and 2) "to make merry over, make sport of."

There are two ways to look at "delight yourself in the Lord and He will give you the desire of your heart." The first is that God changes our desires as we delight ourselves in Him. The second is that God blesses our dreams and desires as we delight in Him (knowing that it would be impossible to continue to take pleasure in God if our desires were destructive or sinful). Both of these have truth in them.

Here is the Backlund expanded version of this verse: "Enjoy yourself in the Lord. <u>Relish</u> in His goodness. <u>Revel</u> in the adventure of walking with Him. <u>Savor</u> every moment with Him. <u>Delight</u> in His unconditional !ove. Get over condemnation, unworthiness, introspection and false humility; and become like a little child in a candy shop with Him." Does this sound too unrealistic? It is not. It is a mindset that can be developed and increased as we get the spirit of religion and performance off of our lives. Again, <u>let's work with God, not for Him</u>.

Another of the Hebrew definitions of "delight" is to be "soft and pliable." This is the opposite of the hardening of our hearts. We keep our hearts soft by developing intimacy with our Lord and by responding with delight, hope and faith when His Word is ministered to us.

Finally, the phrase "dwell in the land, and feed on His faithfulness" needs to be considered. Those who "delight in the Lord" will feed (focus) on the good things He has done. They will seem to go overboard in thinking about and speaking testimonies of God's goodness. They will "gorge" on these and delightfully say, "If He did it then, He will do it again." These people will "dwell" (stay in) the land of proclaiming the faithfulness of God.

Let's delight in the Lord and He will give us the desires of our heart.

Declare: I delight in the Lord. I continually feed on His faithfulness. He gives me the desires of my heart.

Bottom Line Joy

Every Christian will need to "bottom line" God's promises in his or her life. This needs to be done when we are seeking "to stand" for big things in our lives, but there is still major uncertainty and unresolved issues present. It is at this point that we "bottom line" things and say, "No matter what happens, I am going to be okay. God is going to be with me. He is going to take care of me. I release all worry to God. I am going to be fine."

Those who walk in faith can sometimes focus too much on one specific thing happening. This can cause stress and "uptight-ness" as we put "all our eggs in one basket." Certainly we need to believe for particular things, but we also need to have great faith in the overall goodness of God. It is important to relax and say, "I am going to be okay."

Where does joy fit into all of this? It is to be the "oil" that keeps our faith from becoming weird and a burden. If we are not experiencing laughter in our "faith stand", then we are in danger of having a faith without the Hebrews chapter four "rest" that is essential to victory and growth. Joy and laughter are part of this rest.

"Therefore, since a promise remains of entering His rest, let us fear lest any of you seem to have come short of it. . . The word which they heard did not profit them, not being mixed with faith. For we who have believed do enter that rest . . . There remains therefore a rest for the people of God. For he who has entered His rest has himself also ceased from his works as God did from His" (Hebrews 4:1-3a,9-10).

So have you "bottom lined" things lately? Have you taken a deep breath and relaxed during your faith stand? Are you letting rest be the foundation of your faith? These attitudes will make will make all the difference.

Declare: Right now, I say out loud, "It's going to be okay." God is going to take care of me. As I wait for my miracle to manifest, I laugh and stir up joy. I regularly get with others who joyfully help me keep the right perspective in my fight of faith.

Joy Comes in the Morning

"For His anger is but for a moment. His favor is for life. Weeping may endure for a night, but joy comes in the morning" (Psalm 30:5).

Nights represent dark and difficult times of life where it is hard to see clearly. Hope is absent. The night in this verse seems to be tied to "His anger", while the morning is connected with enduring favor. The length of our "night" is influenced greatly by our perception of God's attitude toward us.

Mornings symbolize new beginnings, new hope, new vision and breakthrough. Sometimes, when we are in the depth of the night, we wonder if morning will ever come. It will! Just remember these words, "This too will pass." It is important in our "midnight hour" that we don't make any important decisions or big conclusions. (It is also vital that we have already made it difficult to go back to old comforters and negative life style choices.) Why? Because the morning will come, and joy comes in the morning.

There is one more thing we need to say about all this. The morning will arrive sooner if we learn to arise and shine and stir up joy in the night. Listen to Isaiah. "Arise, shine; for your light has come! And the glory of the LORD is risen upon you. For behold, the darkness shall cover the earth, and deep darkness the people; but the LORD will arise over you, and His glory will be seen upon you" (Isaiah 60:1-2). Paul and Silas did this while in jail. "But at midnight Paul and Silas were praying and singing hymns to God, and the prisoners were listening to them. Suddenly there was a great earthquake, so that the foundations of the prison were shaken; and immediately all the doors were opened and everyone's chains were loosed" (Acts 16:25,26). Paul and Silas brought "morning" to the "night" for others and themselves by worshiping and praising in their midnight hour. Truly, morning came at midnight.

The lies of the enemy sound more real in the night. Let's repel them by focusing on the praises and promises of God in our thoughts, words and songs. It will attract God's glory and ignite "suddenlies" in powerful ways.

Declare: This too will pass. The morning is coming with its great joy. By praise and rejoicing, I am bringing "mornings" to others and to me.

The Song of Celebration and Joy

"When the LORD brought back the captivity of Zion, we were like those who dream. <u>Then our mouth was filled with laughter, and our tongue with singing</u>. Then they said among the nations, 'The LORD has done great things for them.' The LORD has done great things for us, and we are glad" (Psalm 126:1-3).

The Jewish people have a heritage of festiveness in their gatherings. The Old Testament reveals this. "<u>Praise</u> the LORD! Sing to the LORD a new song, and His praise in the assembly of saints. Let Israel <u>rejoice</u> in their Maker; let the children of Zion <u>be joyful</u> in their King. Let them praise His name with the dance; let them sing praises to Him with the timbrel and harp . . . Let the saints be joyful in glory; let them <u>sing aloud</u> on their beds. Let the <u>high praises</u> of God be in their mouth . . . " (Psalm 149:1-6). The heritage of God's people includes joyful celebration in corporate meetings (especially in times of singing together). Unfortunately, Christianity has not always embraced this attitude because of a misconception of the nature of God.

There is something in every one of us that wants and needs to celebrate. Have you every watched a sports team that just won a championship? These athletes (and their fans) leap, raise their arms, run uncontrollably, pile on each other and become like little children in delight. They are rejoicing over a temporal crown.

Jesus <u>has won</u> completely the spiritual championship! (And we are on His team!) He has defeated the devil, sin, sickness, lack and so much more. Great revelation is now being released on the church about this conquest. Wow!

Song services are a great time to celebrate the victory that has already been won. When we combine celebrative music with powerful words, our faith will grow together, and spirits of heaviness and unbelief will fall off of lives. Although celebrative songs are not the only emphasis in our singing, it does need to be a big part as we move from glory to glory, strength to strength and <u>faith to faith</u>.

Declare: I celebrate joyfully the victory of Christ. I sing the high praises of God. I dance. I shout. I love corporate praise gatherings.

DAY #47 *Enemy of Joy: Never Enough*

There is a message that the enemy of our souls repeatedly speaks. It has effectively drained life and joy out of multitudes. These are words that every Christian hears and must learn to overcome. What are these words? Is it a temptation to lie, hate someone, quit reading the Bible or cheat on our spouse? Even though we will hear things like these, he is speaking something even more damaging. It's this: "<u>You aren't doing enough</u>."

Who has not heard things like these: "You haven't prayed or fasted enough. You have not gone long enough without sin? You have not read your Bible enough? You have not forgiven enough? You have not loved your family enough? You have not been consistent enough? You are not sorry enough?" Certainly we have spiritual responsibilities; but if we live in the "never enough" mentality, we have embraced a "works of the law" theology that will actually cut off our flow of grace.

"You have become estranged from Christ, you who attempt to be justified by law; <u>you have fallen from grace</u>. For we through the Spirit eagerly wait for the hope of righteousness by faith. For in Christ Jesus neither circumcision nor uncircumcision avails anything, but <u>faith working through love</u>" (Gal. 5:4-6). In Galatians 5, Paul makes it clear that a <u>works mentality</u> is not only wrong, but causes us to "fall from grace" (to leave the high place of God's empowerment). <u>This disconnection does not occur because we aren't doing enough, but because we have been deceived about what moves the hand of God</u>. It is not doing more that "avails much", but it is "faith working through love." Our focus in life then cannot be on trying to do more to win God's approval, but it needs to be in building a relationship with Him through Jesus so that we trust His goodness (and we realize that Jesus has already done enough).

Our joy is ignited when we have a revelation of what "It is finished" meant (when Jesus spoke this on the cross in John 19:30). Truly, we will enter into a powerful rest when we have "ceased from our own works" (Hebrews 4:10). We may not completely understand what that means (or how to do it), but we can start by answering the "never enough" lie with "Jesus has done enough and I am putting my trust in that today!"

Declare: Jesus has done enough! I rejoice exceedingly in that truth today.

It is requisite for the relaxation of the mind that we make use, from time to time, of playful deeds and jokes. - Thomas Aquinas

Health Benefits of Laughter - Humor Therapy

Humor therapy is the therapeutic process that claims beneficial effects from the positive emotions associated with laughter.

Awareness of humor therapy increased dramatically during the 1970s when Norman Cousins chronicled his experiences of overcoming a serious chronic disease (ankylosing spondylitis - a form of arthritis) by laughing at comedy shows such as "Candid Camera" and "Marx Brothers" films. Cousins stated that ten minutes of laughing gave him two hours of drug-free pain relief.

Research has shown that laughing can help in:

❖ lowering blood pressure
❖ reducing stress hormones.
❖ increasing muscle flexion.
❖ boosting immune function by raising levels of infection-fighting T-cells, disease-fighting proteins called Gammainterferon and B-cells, which produce disease-destroying antibodies.
❖ triggering the release of endorphins, the body's natural painkillers.
❖ producing a general sense of well-being.

Something to Laugh About

A man receives a phone call from his doctor.
The doctor says, "I have some good news and some bad news."
The man says, "OK, give me the good news first."
The doctor says, "The good news is that you have 24 hours to live."
The man replies, "Oh no! If that's the good news, then what's the bad news?"
The doctor says, "The bad news is that I forgot to call you yesterday."

THE FIVE DEVOTIONALS FROM THIS PAST WEEK

Delight Yourself in the Lord
Bottom Line Joy
Joy Comes in the Morning
The Song of Celebration and Joy
Enemy of Joy: Never Enough

TWO ACTIONS TO TAKE:

Read or review each of the week's five devotionals.
Read out loud each of the five declarations at the end of the devotionals.

FOUR QUESTIONS TO ASK:

Which of the five devotionals spoke to you in the greatest way? Why?
What one sentence from the five devotionals stood out to you the most? Why did this speak to you?
How did you do with last week's steps to increase your strength through joy?
What two or three steps can you take this week to move forward in strengthening your life through joy?

FURTHER ACTIONS TO TAKE:

Take time to share lies that you can laugh with each other about (see Day #5).

IF TIME ALLOWS:

Discuss how you are doing in overcoming destination disease (Day #3).
Pray with each other.
Share other thoughts about joy.
Discuss creative ideas of how to walk in greater joy.

Possessing Joy

Week Fight

DAY #50 *Joyfully Seeding the Clouds of the Future (Part 1)*

The Holy Spirit once said to me, "Steve, you often seed the clouds of your future in a negative way and then cry out to me to stop the storm that you have created." God has mercifully answered my prayer many times, but there is a higher way of living.

Imagine with me a cloud over every aspect of your future. It hovers over events coming soon (meetings, ministries, special occasions or just normal life), or it can be over things years ahead. We have the great opportunity to proactively seed the clouds over these happenings. Unfortunately, many plant stormy seeds and then wonder, "How could God have allowed this to happen."

The spirit of foreboding contributes to this seeding with substances that will attract difficulty instead of victory. Anxiety causes many to have harmful belief systems and to speak word curses that sow trouble into the clouds of the days and years ahead. That is a bummer, it is unnecessary and it needs to stop.

In 2 Corinthians 9 we read, "God loves a cheerful (hilarious) giver." This cheerfulness comes from knowing that generosity will seed the clouds of our future. "But this I say: He who sows sparingly will also reap sparingly, and he who sows bountifully will also reap bountifully . . . God loves a cheerful giver. And God is able to make all grace abound toward you, that you, always having all sufficiency in all things, may have an abundance for every good work" (2 Corinthians 9:6-8).

Luke 6:37-38 takes this farther. "Judge not, and you shall not be judged. Condemn not, and you shall not be condemned. Forgive, and you will be forgiven. Give, and it will be given to you: good measure, pressed down, shaken together, and running over will be put into your bosom. For with the same measure that you use, it will be measured back to you." **Incredibly, we can proactively seed our clouds to whatever measure we want**, which will bring future "rain" in proportion to our sowing. Now that is something to get cheerful about!

Declare: God is empowering me to increasingly sow cheerfully into the clouds of my future through thanksgiving, proactive words, thoughts, actions, forgiveness, love and a growing relationship with Jesus.

DAY #51 *Joyfully Seeding the Clouds of the Future (Part 2)*

Here is something I want you to try. Ask a friend to count backwards in his mind from 10 to 1. In the middle of him doing this, ask him to say his name out loud. What happened to their mental counting when they spoke? Unless he has two brains, the counting stopped. Hmm. What meaneth this? It's this: We cannot think the old thought <u>while speaking</u> God's truth, and <u>speaking truth</u> ultimately helps create new thoughts and attitudes

A first step in warring against lies in our thinking is to capture them and replace them with God's promises. Every <u>overcoming Christian</u> has to develop this habit, but we also need to understand that changing our thinking (repenting) is not just done mentally. It is speeded up by getting into the habit of <u>speaking truth and faith</u> into our lives and into our future.

As we learned in the last devotional, we "seed" the clouds over our future through our beliefs, our words, our prayers and our actions. Our thoughts (beliefs) primarily will cause spiritual rain or drought. That is why we vigilantly replace hopelessness, worry and unloving attitudes. Most people however find that simply warring in the mind is not enough to uproot old strongholds and to establish new positive strongholds of hope, joy, love and faith. This is why <u>speaking truth</u> is a key to breaking old mental struggles.

Here is a powerful step to take. Take different areas of your future (i.e. ministry, health, finances, family, vocation, relationships, protection, evangelism, your nation, your church, miracles, etc.) and spend specific time "seeding" the cloud over this aspect of life. For instance, focus on your vocation for two minutes and say things like: "Thank you God that I am blessed in my employment. Thank you that my honesty, creativity, dependability, enthusiasm, and personal blessing create great success for this business and in every business that I will ever be a part of. I will never lack a good job because of how big my God is in me. Jesus has made me successful and I continually make others successful." Then take additional areas of life and do the same thing. It will ultimately create a "storm" of blessing and godly influence.

Declare: I have a plan to seed the clouds of my future so I joyfully speak God's promises into my life.

DAY #52 *I Rejoice At Your Word As One Who Finds Great Treasure* (Psalm 119:162)

Can you imagine the joy of finding "great treasure" in your back yard or in a nearby cave? How would you respond to this? Most likely, you would be wildly and positively emotional and probably leap for joy. Why? Because something in you would understand that this undeserved good fortune would radically change your life. Indeed, it would be impossible to contain your joy.

The psalmist said, "I rejoice at Your Word as one who finds great treasure." Can you picture him doing so? He is celebrating because he realizes that God's Word (His promises) is more valuable than any earthly treasure that could be found.

God's Word releases wisdom. "<u>Happy</u> is the man who finds wisdom, and the man who gains understanding; For her proceeds are better than the profits of silver, and her gain than fine gold. She is more precious than rubies, <u>And all the things you may desire cannot compare with her</u>. Length of days is in her right hand, in her left hand riches and honor. Her ways are ways of pleasantness, and all her paths are peace. She is a tree of life to those who take hold of her, and happy are all who retain her" (Proverbs 3:13-18).

<u>God's Word also leads us to joyous intimacy with our creator through Jesus Christ</u>. "Then Jesus said . . . , 'If you abide in My word, you are My disciples indeed. And you shall <u>know the truth</u>, and the truth shall make you free'" (John 8:31,32). "Knowing" is a word with deep meaning that includes intimacy. With that in mind, it is important to understand that truth is more than a way of believing; but it is a person, Jesus Christ. Jesus said, "I am . . . the truth . . . No one comes to the Father except through Me" (John 14:6). God's Word must lead to a deeper relationship with the Father, or else we do not truly "know truth"; but probably are just becoming religious.

God's Word brings great joy through its wisdom and by fueling our love affair with Jesus. Let's spend time in the Scriptures every day. Let's meditate on it day and night. Let's fellowship with others in the Word. Truly, we will rejoice exceedingly as we do.

Declare: God, I rejoice at Your Word as one who finds great treasure. I love the Bible. I love hearing Your Word preached and taught.

Derek Prince in his book, <u>Blessings or Curses – You Can Choose</u>, teaches on "The Great Exchange" that took place on the cross. It is a powerful teaching about the magnificence of our salvation. He shares that Jesus, through His sinless life, "deserved" life (by fulfilling the law); but we, because of sin, deserve death. Jesus "took" our death on the cross and offers His life to us in exchange. We can receive this by grace through faith. (This is why the gospel is "good news"!)

There are seven other "exchanges" that are offered to us. He took the punishment we deserve and offers us the forgiveness He deserves; He took our sickness and offers us His divine health; our poverty for His riches; our rejection for His acceptance; our sin for His righteousness; our curses for His blessing; and, finally, our shame for His glory.

It is shame that we want to focus on. Shame is a negative emotion that is made up of feelings of dishonor, unworthiness and embarrassment. It is a strong enemy of joy and victorious living. Shame results from an acute awareness of our own poor choices, or it comes from things that have happened to us that cause us to feel unworthy. If we are going to mature in our relationship with Jesus, the plague of shame and unworthiness must be defeated.

Jesus took our shame when He hung naked and fully exposed on the cross. Not only did this occur, but more importantly Jesus took all of our shame on Himself as He died (just as He took our sin, punishment, rejection, sickness, poverty, curses, etc.). Hebrews 12 helps us to see this. "Looking unto Jesus, the author and finisher of our faith, who for the joy that was set before Him endured the cross, <u>despising the shame</u>, and has sat down at the right hand of the throne of God" (Hebrews 12:2).

If we unconsciously feel that we don't deserve to be happy, then shame and unworthiness have a hold on us. Let's do all we can to make things right with God and people, but then move onto a life where "the joy of the Lord is our strength" (Neh. 8:10). Let's break out of our past. <u>Others need us to be strong</u>.

Declare: Jesus took my shame. I am worthy to receive all of God's blessings, including being outrageously joyful. My hope and joy are rising up just as Christ rose from the dead!

In the parable of the talents (Matthew 25:14-30), the master applauds the two faithful servants and says to each, "Well done, good and faithful servant; you were faithful over a few things, I will make you ruler over many things. <u>Enter into the joy of your lord</u>" (Matthew 25:21,23). This verse promises eternal rewards for faithfulness and for the improving of what we have been given; but it also gives insight into how we can step into greater favor, into greater open doors and into increased spiritual influence here on earth.

Jesus said, "I will <u>make you</u> ruler over many things." He said that He would make us this. It is interesting that He would follow up this promise with a command, "Enter into the joy of your lord." Could there be a link between our "entering into joy" and His "making us ruler over many things"? I believe there is.

Psalms 100:4 gives us further insight: "Enter into His gates with thanksgiving, and into His courts with praise. Be thankful to Him, and bless His name." This verse is a map that leads us into new dimensions in God. We enter into these new levels through an increase of thanksgiving to God and people. We will proceed to the "headwaters" of these truths and experiences by turning our thanksgiving into praise (a higher quality of thanksgiving which focuses on the goodness of God's nature).

When we put thanksgiving and praise together, we have a lot of joy. This joy reflects a radical trust in God, and it also is evidence of a deep soul prosperity that releases "many things" like spiritual authority, influence, physical health, and abundant provision. "Beloved, I pray that you may prosper in all things and be in health, just as your soul prospers" (3 John 2).

I have a word for you. <u>Enter into the joy of your Lord</u>. Move forward in this elevated aspect of living by increasing your thankfulness and praise. Make a decision that you are going to find the keys to the joy of the Lord, and then persevere in walking in them. <u>This is a hidden door for those who are answering the call to take on greater kingdom responsibility in the days ahead</u>.

Declare: I am increasingly faithful with the small things of my life and God is now increasing my influence so His kingdom can expand. To walk in this, I am entering into the joy of my Lord.

Joy does not simply happen to us. We have to choose joy and keep choosing it every day. - Henri Nouwen

Health Benefits of Laughter - Losing weight by laughing

There are people who use laughter as a means to lose weight. And this is no joke! Intentional laughing is a discipline for more and more people.

Individuals are gathering together to laugh out loud at thousands of "laugh clubs" around the world. "Laughter therapy" is becoming part of the treatment plan at more and more hospitals, and there is a new exercise movement called Laughtercising that is emerging to assist with weight loss.

Katie Namrevo wrote a book in 2004 called Laugh It Off! Weight Loss for the Fun of It. She believes that her own experience is proof that laughter will help others shed the pounds. On the back cover of her book is a "before" photo showing her as an out of shape 50-year-old, and then an "after" photo when she is 54-year-old after she laughed off 35 pounds.

Namrevo says she was a "stress eater" who had tried many diets and pills to reduce weight. One day, after watching a TV program on laughter therapy, she headed to her refrigerator to "medicate" and decided to try laughing loud and hard instead. She continued this and kept laughing between thirty seconds and five minutes up to ten times a day. As she did, her cravings stopped. She also said she began losing weight, had more energy and developed a desire to exercise.

Something to Laugh About Bulletin Bloopers

Ladies, don't forget the rummage sale. It's a chance to get rid of those things not worth keeping around the house. Don't forget your husbands.

Remember in prayer the many that are sick of our community. Smile at someone who is hard to love. Say "hell" to someone who doesn't care much about you.

Day #56 *Let's Now Continue in Joy*

THE FIVE DEVOTIONALS FROM THIS PAST WEEK
Joyfully Seeding the Clouds of the Future (Part 1)
Joyfully Seeding the Clouds of the Future (Part 2)
I Rejoice at Your Word As One Who Finds Great Treasure
Enter Into the Joy of Your Lord
Enemy of Joy: Shame and Feeling Unworthy

TWO ACTIONS TO TAKE:
Read or review each of the week's five devotionals
Read out loud each of the five declarations at the end of the
devotionals

FOUR QUESTIONS TO ASK:
Which of the five devotionals spoke to you in the greatest
way? Why?
What one sentence from the five devotionals stood out to you
the most? Why did this speak to you?
How did you do with last week's steps to increase your
strength through joy?
What can you do to keep growing in joy now that you have
finished this book? What is your action plan to not lose the
ground you have gained?

FURTHER ACTIONS TO TAKE:
One last time - laugh at some lies

IF TIME ALLOWS:
Discuss how you are doing in overcoming destination disease
(Day #3).
Pray with each other.
Share other thoughts about joy.
Discuss creative ideas of how to walk in greater joy.

Appendix I

Day #2 from Steve & Wendy Backlund's book
Igniting Faith in 40 Days

A Lying Apple Tree?
Calling those things that are not . . . (Rom 4:17)

An apple tree will produce apples because of what it is. When it is young, it will have no apples; but it still must say, "I am an apple tree." When it is winter and there are no leaves or apples; it still says, "I am an apple tree." Is it lying at those times? No. It would be lying to say anything different.

Many Christians have a hard time saying who God says they are when no fruit is manifesting in that particular area. Could they be "too young" in that truth to be fruitful? Could they be in a season where that dimension of the Christian life is being pruned back for future growth? Either way, it does not mean they are lying when they say, "I am anointed, prosperous, delivered, healed, righteous, strong etc."

Joel 3:10 says, "Let the weak say I am strong." We don't deny the fact of weakness, but we focus on the greater truth that we are strong in Him.

Again, because the Word says we ARE these things, we would be untruthful to say anything different. Let's not lie against the truth. Indeed we ARE what the Bible says we are.

Declare: I am who the Word says I am. I have a sound mind. I have great favor with God and man. People love me. I am a happy person. I love life and enjoy every day. I am healed. I have abundant provision. I am blessed and protected. I increasingly know who and what I am in Christ. I make a tremendous difference for Christ wherever I go.

Appendix 2

Day #3 from Steve & Wendy Backlund's book
<u>Igniting Faith in 40 Days</u>

Bringing Life to Dead Places
Let the weak say "I am strong" (Joel 3:10)

God has called us to make "dead things" alive. In Ezekiel 37, the prophet was asked if the dry bones could live. In the dialogue and events that followed, God showed Ezekiel and His people a powerful principle that is vital for us today.

God's method of bringing life to these "very dry" bones was through Ezekiel prophesying "life" to the whole situation. Ezekiel had to speak to the bones. He had to prophesy to the wind. As he did, things changed and life came.

You and I also must continually speak to dead areas in our lives and circumstances. A main "method" of God bringing change to a situation is for one of His children to speak His promises over people and circumstances. "And God who gives life to the dead and calls those things that are not as though they are" (Romans 4:17).

It starts with each of us prophesying "life" over ourselves. Joel gives us a good place to start in Joel 3:10, "Let the weak say I am strong." Start now a life long habit to "call those things that are not as though they are" in your life.

Declare: Even though I feel weak at times, I am really strong. I am very strong to accomplish God's purpose in my life and to be a strength to others. I prophesy daily over my circumstances, my future, and over the dry areas of my life.

Appendix 3

Day #10 from Steve & Wendy Backlund's book
<u>Igniting Faith in 40 Days</u>

Who Do You Think You Are! (Part 2)
Calling those things that are not, as though they were
(Romans 4:17)

Here is a major life question: Does our experience create our identity or does our identity create our experience? The answer is . . . (drum roll please) . . . our identity creates our experience. Remember, those who think they can, and those who think they can't, are both right (consider the spies in Numbers 13 and 14). What we believe about ourselves will either bind us or launch us.

When it comes to who we think we are, God is calling us to believe His Word instead of negative experiences. He says "Consider yourselves dead to sin, but alive to God . . . " (Romans 6:11), and "Let the weak say I am strong" (Joel 3:10). Abraham "did not consider his own body, already dead . . ." (Romans 4:19).

Satan, on the other hand, wants us to focus on our failures and lack. A battle rages in our souls concerning what to believe about ourselves. Do we "call ourselves" by our negative experience or by God's promise. Proverbs 23:7 declares "As (a man) thinks in his heart, so is he." Let's think God's thoughts about us, and not anything else.

Declare: I am a new creation in Christ. Old things have passed away. All things are new. I am strong in Christ. I am who the Bible says I am.

Cracks in the Foundation
Another Book by Steve Backlund

What Bill Johnson Says About This Book

In his great book, Cracks in the Foundation, Steve goes beyond adding life to old thoughts; he successfully inspires the reader to take another look at common ideas that have gone unchallenged for far too long. In doing so, he builds a biblically based foundation of understanding that is very significant. In fact, I believe this foundation is necessary for us to fully embrace the reformation that is at hand. This is a book that I wish every Christian would read.

Bill Johnson, Author, International Speaker
Redding, CA

From the Introduction of _Cracks in the Foundation_

This is a book that challenges many of the "basic assumptions" of familiar Bible verses and other common phrases. It is designed to help you think through what you believe. It has the potential to "fill" and repair many "cracks" in our thinking that rob us of potential. You may not agree with everything written, but I believe that you will be motivated to go to a higher level in "nailing down" your own beliefs about the key issues that are raised in _Cracks in the Foundation_.

Verses and phrases studied in _Cracks in the Foundation_:

#1	If it be your will
#2	All things work together for good
#3	He . . . sends rain on the just and on the unjust
#4	It is appointed unto men once to die
#5	God is in control
#6	The answer to your prayer will be yes, no or wait
#7	God is sovereign
#8	We must be balanced in our Christian walk
#9	But the prince of the kingdom of Persia withstood me twenty-one days
#10	It is God who heals the sick, not me

More verses and phrases studied in *Cracks in the Foundation*:

#11	Every time I minister or move forward in God, Satan attacks me
#12	Give to him who asks you
#13	Do good . . . hoping for nothing in return
#14	Do all speak with tongues?
#15	A thorn in the flesh was given to me
#16	I am claiming my healing by faith
#17	All religions have truth in them
#18	Will you pray for my healing?
#19	What about Job?
#20	The love of money is the root of all kinds of evil
#21	We will never fully understand the mysterious ways of God
#22	Spiritual warfare is mainly dealing with the devil
#23	The Lord gives and the Lord takes away
#24	God will do it in His time
#25	The greatest among you will be your servant
#26	All Christians must go through a personal wilderness or desert experience
#27	You did not have enough faith to be healed
#28	We are living in the last days
#29	God won't override someone's free will
#30	All who desire to live godly in Christ Jesus will suffer persecution
#31	The anointing of God sets people free
#32	No man can control the tongue
#33	We don't need to be part of a church to be a Christian
#34	It's not about me
#35	Let all things be done decently and in order
#36	God helps those who help themselves
#37	Sincerity & having a good heart are the most important things in the Christian life
#38	People close to God are misunderstood and struggle in relationships with people
#39	And every branch that bears fruit He prunes
#40	God is going to kill you
#41	Partial obedience is not obedience
#42	Calling those things that don't exist as though they did

GO TO ignitedhope.com FOR ORDERING INFORMATION

Printed in Great Britain
by Amazon.co.uk, Ltd.,
Marston Gate.